Blueberries and Apricots

poems

Natasha Kanapé Fontaine

translated by
HOWARD SCOTT

MAWENZI
HOUSE

We acknowledge the support of the Canada Council for the Arts for our publishing program. We also acknowledge support from the Government of Ontario through the Ontario Arts Council.

We acknowledge the financial support of the Government of Canada through the National Translation Program for Book Publishing, an initiative of the *Roadmap for Canada's Official Languages 2013-2018: Education, Immigration, Communities*, for our translation activities.

Previously published in a French edition as *Bleuets et abricots* by Mémoire d'encrier, Montreal, Quebec.

Cover design by Sabrina Pignataro

Library and Archives Canada Cataloguing in Publication
Kanapé Fontaine, Natasha, 1991-
[Bleuets et abricots. English]
Blueberries and apricots : poems / Natasha Kanapé Fontaine ; translated by Howard Scott.
Translation of: Bleuets et abricots.
Issued in print and electronic formats.
ISBN 978-1-988449-32-6 (softcover).--ISBN 978-1-988449-33-3 (HTML)
I. Scott, Howard, 1952-, translator II. Title. III. Title: Bleuets et abricots. English.
PS8621.A49B5313 2018 C841'.6 C2018-901878-X
C2018-901879-8

Printed and bound in Canada by Coach House Printing

Mawenzi House Publishers Ltd.
39 Woburn Avenue (B)
Toronto, Ontario M5M 1K5
Canada
www.mawenzihouse.com

And we are standing up now, my country and I, hair in the wind, my hand now in its huge fist and the strength is not in us, but above us, in a voice that pierces the night and the hearing like the penetrance of an apocalyptic wasp. And the voice proclaims that for centuries Europe has force-fed us with lies and bloated us with pestilence.

AIMÉ CÉSAIRE

PROLOGUE

A cry rises in me and transfigures me. The world waits for woman to come back as she was born: woman standing, woman powerful, woman resurgent. A call rises in me and I've decided to say yes to my birth.

I am because I am. I say I. I know how to give life. I am fertile. The poem enters me like a lover. The universe enters my body to continue the movement of the life cycle. Everything is circle. The land. The blueberries and the apricots. The poem is the movement that fertilizes.

I am the poem of existence.

I feel everything. The memories. The wounds. I see everything. The shock of dispossession. To speak up and ease the burden. The weight of pain. I write to say yes. To me. Woman. Force open the doors of silence. Maintain the path. Give back life to the shadows, to the broken children, to the words that no longer know how to say yes. That no longer know how to keep standing. That no longer know how to keep the word.

I speak to the wind and to the sea. I am cannibal priestess. Eater of horizons. I offer the sea a basket of food.

I remember . . .

NATASHA KANAPÉ FONTAINE

FIRST MOVEMENT

The body lent to me
is the temple of my soul.
May I be judged by the fruits
that fall from my tree.

SAMIAN

THE WALK

I begin my
circumpolar
walk

From our feet we wipe
the rain of the tropics
the sand of the sea
I remember
the salt of the St Lawrence
necklace on my mother's neck

I remember
the silt
land of mine
my flesh

Equal to the burnt planet
I will spew a last cry
to human suffering:
the birth of myself
the thunderbird

Land of mine oh
I will call you by your name
to the gates Anticosti
to the gates Eeyou Istchee
open the door
to refugees

We will gather
the invisible wealth
lost between the cities
will chain up the monsters of history
the eternal stories of civilization
in our subarctic forests

Land of mine oh
I will make myself beautiful for the poem
of my grandmother

If I named you my belly
if I named you my face
the name of my mountains my river
Utshuat Upessamiu Shipu
the name of my river my sand my lichen
Uinipek^{u} Nutshimit

I will do my hair
like an Arctic reindeer
like the resinous moss of the spruces
water of life of the gatherings

I remember
the peat hands damp
submissive to despair
to desire

Land of mine oh
here is your name
nestled among my guts
sand and beaches
moon and stones

Chief of wandering
vibrant clearings
stormy taigas
tundras of turmoil
you call yourself savage
you seep into my flesh
inside

Your name emerges
body of foam
lying on the shore
stones open to the sea
the tectonic plates
surge inside me
nature has made you so well
the limestone ringing
under my robes
first female

Homage to life
homage to love

I say I
to say the others
the suffering of my people
hills and rivers
rising and setting
shaped by the Perseids
promises of dawn

Reaching
my archipelago
slaughtered story

I have never
wanted to be a slave
I refuse forever

We have never wanted
to be slaves
to drunkenness I refuse forever

Burn me
hang me
as much as you want
as much as history will repeat
I will come back a hundredfold

I am queen
my sacrifice will raise me
fire and tree
where you have hung my remains
they will answer you
tin horns and drums
thunder and tornado

Exile embraces
the infinity of the flood

Many hurricanes will traverse the earth
day after day
people land of mine
forest roads
clouds of yesterday and tomorrow

We will retranscribe the wayward prayers
those to come
we will fulfill the ancestral lullabies
murmuring from above and from below

We will have to raise the torch to the dawn
the stone pierces
the mystery and the memory
the road is old
it is memory of time
fossil of our words

The sky will kneel
striated with whitish scars
sink to the heart of the planet
take joy in the vitality
of the cosmos

The songs of peace will burst forth
we will see the flowers land of mine
on the freed hair of our girls
Louis Riel will come back laughing
among the horses and deer
the buffalo will run again
on the lands

Manito Ahbee

Take pity on me
Nitassinan
I pray.

First massacres of our clans
I still shed
the tears of grieving
the sighs of shame

I have memory of death
kiss the knowledge on my forehead
the return of my people guided by the shadows

I am woman the land
from which my name was taken
my pubis awaits the coming
the missionaries called me Montagnaise
I say territory woman
my mountains will teach you the future

A woman will rise
dressed in her lichen robe
dressed in her traditions
dressed in her inner drum

She will be standing
in front of the machines
territorial mystery
a breeze
will brush your necks
it's wind in my head, you'll say

I'll repeal every law
in the country that men invent
you will learn

Land of mine has a bigger name
than America.

THE HUNT

Here

Eyes looking to four directions
I am nothing other than a woman

Woman among women and men
woman between Moon and Sun
woman between Earth and Sky

Here
I probe the space
cardinal after cardinal
I am born in the world

The past and the future call me
ultimate vibrations
on missing notes
the symphony orchestra
climbs my thighs like pink salmons
sweet water of return

My tongue
eel
between jargons and borders
I stammer

No one will see the light
in front of the people
the wind rises greater
Kanata land of mine

Permeate the tundra with your odour
my hair on your chest
will change into stems
between sky and land
trees and roots

I will raise my arms toward the moon
my eyes toward the sun
laugh in chorus with our parents
the canoes on the oceans
those stone reeds
with you between my thighs

I am Indigenous woman
you know it now
I will kiss
the light the world
I will be in my most beautiful day of pleasuring

The trout dances
from stream to stream
from river to river
from village to village
nothing more touches the dawn

Now I know how to write
now I know how to speak up
now I know your tongue
I sing your syllables

I will cancel the new beginning
I will close the circle
with my mouth and my teeth

I will stop grinding my jaw
I will cradle the future
Kanata

Here goes

Your genesis is called village

I am earth woman
first pushes
from which you draw your birth

I will kiss you ravenously
remember the taste of the earth
I will drown the word with my saliva
remember the taste of the river
I had made you my confessions
I am big and beautiful like an eel

You will no longer glorify me
you'll see that I know how to speak
you'll learn to be quiet
I'll eat your tongue

You will no longer glorify me
I will be neither Statue of Liberty
neither voodoo doll nor festive pomp
I will take human form

I will put my fingers
in the hollow of my ear
will kiss your temples

neck and head
will put my leg on your hips
heat up your passions
your forehead on my shoulder
the cold of your hands

I remember
pierced by the lance that killed Christ
Bible passages

I crossed on dry ground
the depressions in the path
I kept the Word of God
to save my soul
I quoted whole passages
I would throw out those words
to build my freedom

I would throw that book
from my Nukum's hands
my Nimushum
and caribou Atik^{u}

That book laid down a hundred times
on my abdomen
read a thousand times the psalms
dreamt of David
waited for Isaiah Jeremiah Ezekiel
the priest hid his right hand
under my white skirt
first communion

They took my grandmother's language
she drank the liquor of the missals
she stopped drinking anything else
the wine of Sunday mass
the children grew up
in the dark rooms
houses where you learned to lie

The pages opened up
to sand and earth
there was the word salt
and the salt was scattered in the minds

I threw some over my left shoulder
they say that if you look back at the city
you'll be turned into a pillar of stone

The salt opened the blood of our children
the sugar ground our nerves
the milk crushed our bones

I have eaten the book
I have rebirthed my grandmother
I have rebirthed my birth

Today I'm drunk
my pain is dulled
the animals don't know how to say
mercury
I drink the source of the storm
the dams are my chains
the brown rum quenches my thirst
I swear by the name of the cane

my canoe overturned my ridicule
my pillaged hills my gold

I remember
the first deportees
the burnt sun of the Antilles
I go back against the current
the temples of sacrifice
the glorious beaches

Open me up
I have no reserve
I did not know how to unbind
either your words or your beginning
my cemeteries are full

Here we are advancing
straight to the void
the boundary of the North
sculpted man
constraining
destiny

Divert the river
from its course
music of the falls
the water promises minerals memory
equilibrium elevation

It changes beds at the rapids
and the lament of the whales
the trucks run
big bears of sorrow

from the woods where they plant machinery
century after century
orgies of kings
abandoning behind them
broken landscape
broken bones
my broken caribou trot

Divert the river from its course
the cliffs land of mine
greed will have led to
the separation of the waters
prophecy in those old stories of Exodus

I lean toward the South
the pain turns to bites
my sick left rib
can no longer wait for the wolf's teeth

I have no more mirror
to recognize my face
the thirst in my throat
in my convictions
in our cries

The tips of my fingers
the juice of pomegranates
forgotten taste of mangos
I stand at the mouth of edens
lips sweetened by apricots
finally drink from the sea
the flavour of your foreign tongue

I walk to the South

I feed on blueberries and apricots
the shores don't answer each other
I have to speak for the beginning
I have to cook up jams
I will eat the blue skin of the berries
to keep my warmth
I will give fruits
to the cold
to learn the name
of my country

I run barefoot toward the shore
in the hot sand of the North
I pierced the sea
you stopped at the edge
do you remember

Bewitched
I try again to entice you between the waters
so you'll come to drink the pleasure of a fresh berry
so you'll come to drink the pleasure of another body
so you'll come taste land of mine
with your whole being

Our nights are the nights of the ends of the earth
once there were countless stars
they guided my son
mouth to suckle on the breast of the Way
I see walking there the Bears and the Archer
I scream I weep

my story is built on the trail of the Perseids
I find you hair tangled
you my son my husband
my dream my mirage

Inseparable from my folly

Give me the word of the sea
give me the origin of the world
give me the vomit of the river
give me the dead bodies of birds

Give me the anthem of the gods of Africa
give me the anaconda of Mami Wata
give me the ghost of the black eagle
give me the jaguar's teeth

I will make flames for joy
I will make games for love

I will give them to Voodoo gods

I will beg for the ibo
I will beg for the nago
I will beg for the petro

I will fabricate the rara of the *soley*
they will see themselves burning their gold chains
at the centre of the makusham
great circle of the feast

My son is dead long live the son

My obvious irrepressible thirsts
my Cartier's ways of the cross
my tongue burnt with drinking from the
black sands of the Athapaskan

I immolated myself
on the pyres of the machines
crows fall by thousands
the holy word intoxicated by the factories

I threw myself down from high
atop drilling stations
I attuned my skin to the Arctic
the Majestic, Sedna without fingers
I've forgotten the name of the tides
that the ice people gave his mother
I swam as far as my memory

My son is dead long live the son

He has the black eyes of my water lover
he has the golden skin of our Eloi people
he has the riches of *Zile*
he has the power of his archipelago
he is smaller than my tibia
awake the dawn from its lethargy
put to sleep the son who doesn't know how to cry

My son is dead long live the son

We have seen Columbus
González
Guerrero
Cortés
Ovando

We gave them yellow gold
the orchestra the dance and the ripe poems
palm leaves and star fruits

We have eaten the conquistadors
to better drink the water of the sea

For the sacrifice of Agwe Tawoyo.

GATHERING

In the North the stars race by
the northern lights keep watch
give me back the names of those waterways
dried up by dams
so I can drink the water from our mountains
with the kiss of his mouth

We braid our hair again
no one to scalp it now
tear it out

We braid the sweetgrass
hair of our mother earth
we burn it for the skies
we listen to the cantilenas
of dawn and the sea
the seventh generation rises
they count the stars
in the dark shadows
and black holes
they know by heart the names of the galaxies
of the solar systems
the star people

My heart throbs
I slip rings
onto my fingers
I put a golden jewel on my head
tonight, I'll dress

in my lichen robe
I'll fix my hair
when the drum man comes
I'll whisper in his ear
a thousand secrets
about meteors

I want the warmth
of a solar eclipse
signal on my skin
geometric tattoo
to construct
the coming time

He comes to gather me
in my belly
here grow the blueberries
that we will harvest
on our festive day
we'll have to
take care of them

The blue flowers will open
to name perpetual summer
between the fingers of a child
to tell the time of tasting the ripe berry
that spreads its nectar over the river

I walk to the South
I came into the world
before Montreal

They spoke, humans
animals vegetables
they travelled, humans
animals vegetables

Hochelaga crossroads island
where cultures and languages drink each other

I know how to track down
blueberries and apricots

Montreal
look up
remember your name
Hochelaga

My people is a people of clouds
we don't shovel them in winter
the snow raises us like rebels
snowshoes on our feet, high cheekbones
fir tree honey on our lips

Guided by the snows
the ice ages our space
we are worthy
we are living

I savour the cumulus clouds
concrete buildings wooden fences
I have to stretch my neck

I sip the cirrus clouds
the others speak
another language
another way of thinking
another way of living

The horizon has a name
here
that I don't know

where have
the broad visions gone
eyes embedded
in the depths?

The horizon
fruit of orgasm
far off the lover hurtles down
the slopes

The horizon
ripe fruit
twilight blueberry
for the first kiss

Will apricots fallen from the tree
know the feeling of being eaten?
of entering the body
of knowing the tongue
the saliva
the taste

Embrace destiny
the quest
penetrate the arteries
to the bones
to the marrow
certainty
of having freed
your fullness

I will open
the gate land of mine
the gate to the South
I will open the gate to Les Abricots
the Eden of Indians

I shout
everything sprouts
and shoots up

Montreal
look up
Montreal
remember your name
Hochelaga

I
have come to shut
the gates of the Plan Nord
the gates of death

I say
Tundra
I say
Nutshimit

I am the Woman of Space
a red and black hat
covers my hair

Coil my hair
around my ears

I am the Woman of Space
thirsty for horizons
I am free
and I am captive
my mother spoke this way
I am the Woman of Space
please gather me
before I fall from the tree
and roll too far

A sweet tongue will say to all ears
Mwen fou pou li
Tshetshue nitshishkueikun, tshetshue nishatshiau
my arteries will drain my blood
fever rising
my breasts swell
my vulva swells
excites the fruit the desire
just to see the break of day
with the feeling of being full

he'll come
to me
the beloved
to swell my dreams

Now that I wear the beaded hat
I speak my dreams
my visions
my hopes

I recognize my people here
indigenous woman
cheeky woman
territory woman
black earth woman
pleasure woman

Give birth to the light
the star will embrace the dawns
give birth to the clearings
give birth to the great bears

Clearing
I am
generation woman
nation amidst nations
upright
naked
stripped bare
breasts skyward
I say I
I am

And you're already drooling
just glimpsing me
there is only your desire
that stands up

You won't have my track
nor my print
asphalt roads
my print
you will carry it in your blood
you will carry it in your marrow

Where did you drop your virtue?
where did you lose your people?

I hear you cough
I climb down from my burning stake
—they called me a witch—
from the cross in the schools
I will give you my breast
you will drink my milk
from my left nipple

I no longer remember your name
I hide my face in my hands
spell me the name of my land
spell me the name of my mother
my eyelids have been closed
for too many centuries.

Will you also offer me these gold jewels
to shackle my wrists?

My name was invented by revolt.

On my right hip
a basket of fruits
dream of being
boat

a boat
the people inside
women and children first

blueberries apricots
on the cobblestones
of the hot city

On my left hip
a face

I walk
I walk upright
like a shadow

a people on my hip
a boatload of fruit
and the dream inside
women and children first

I write a poem
on the hip of dawn

the dawn that I imagine
hanging from my breasts
the mouth
of my lover

a night a dream
my son I will say to him
you have to find
the road again

to the feet
of your mother

My son
fell asleep
at my nipple

the sand pillow
carries his dreams
to the native country

my pain
soothed by the waters
that carry away
the bodies of our daughters

my wounds
healed by
the herbs of my land

where is the water
I will drink
to survive

Blueberries and apricots

still life
recitative for a shadow

we are beached
on the floor of martyr bears.

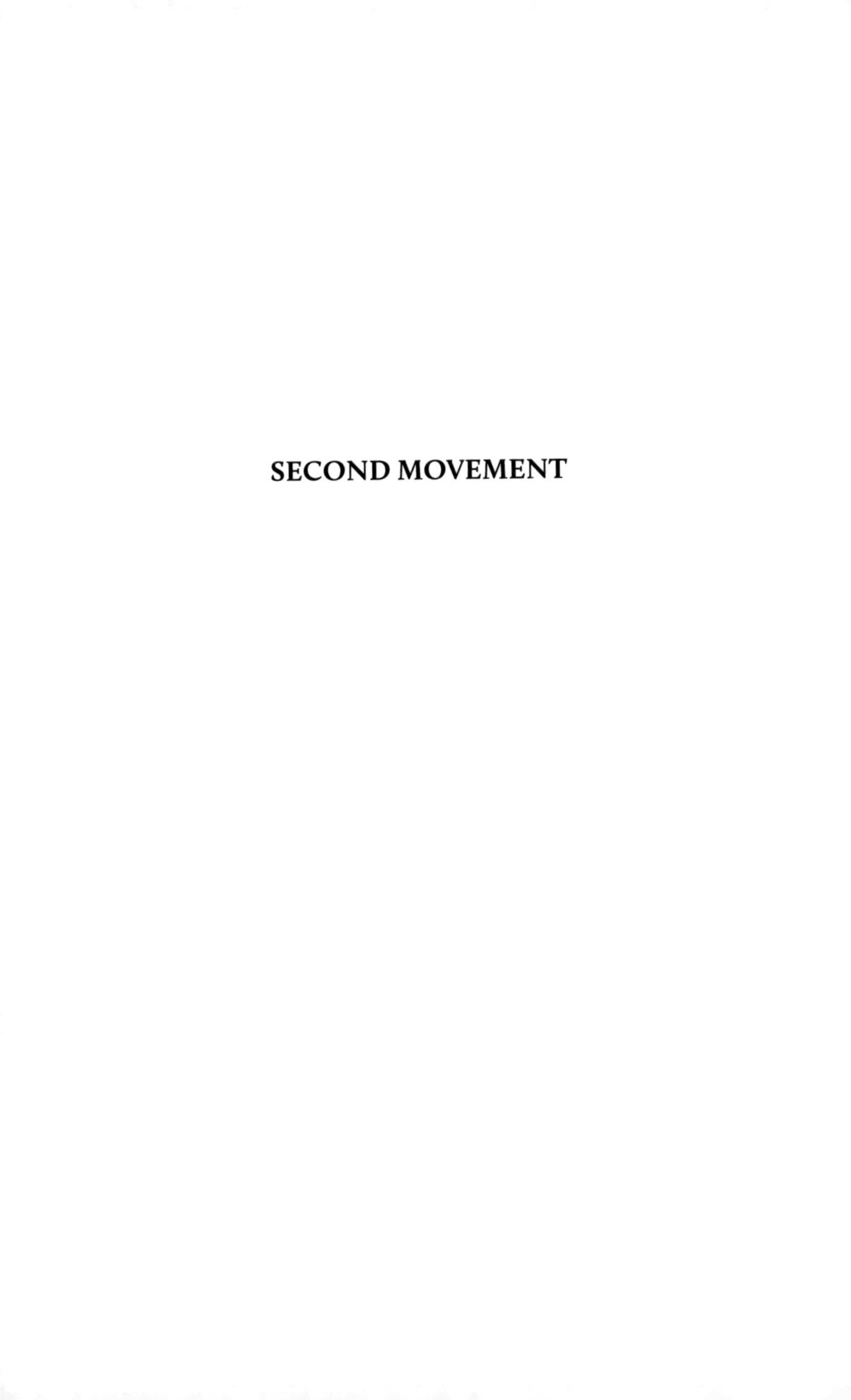

SECOND MOVEMENT

It cried in the evening, the earth. Dry tears dispersed in the slightest breeze, scattered to the four winds. It hurt your eyes, the earth. It went into your nose, it went into your throat and choked you, the earth. Day and night, for months, it was dying, abandoning men to idleness, thus condemning itself to forced rest.

JEAN-CLAUDE FIGNOLÉ

THE RESERVE

You will no longer glorify me

You will steal the verb pray
you will deny the day
when I'll grip the weapon
to set my mutation in motion
you'll aim your land army
to irritate my bones
buried under your authority
golf courses and pine groves

You will see
border crossings fall
cars in reverse
fire pillaging
the fields of corn

You will swallow
my red pomegranates
my cranberries
my salmon my trout
our smoked angers
you will taste my joy
fruit of bitterness
sweet sap of revolt

I will remember

You will push back my bodies my borders
you will burn the trunks of pine of birch

I'll sob a refrain
old territory litany
the father of my father

You will stone my people
kill one of their fathers
come to speak to our angers
no one will lend an ear
to the terrors of keeping silent
at his mother's breasts

We will rise
scarves on our faces
red on our lips
ancient symbols on our backs
I will right the doors of the future
throw out the shutters of the reserves
open my village to the world

We will rise
we will burn the schools
our children become forebears
our forebears become children

I will contrive between my thighs
the formula of orality
redemption
our island

We will learn the name of the earth.

Listen to the world
collapsing
concrete bridges
asphalt roads

Aho for joy
Aho for love

Arises woman
fists clenched
toward the light

Here come migrating
the peoples without lands
we will rewrite war
unique fable

Who can win over lies
build an empire of victors
and believe it without limit

That which poisons
will not deserve to live
that which wounds will not deserve the clan
five hundred years later
seven generations after

All those broken window frames blocking the roads
all those walls erected between nations
all those boatloads of slaves
those oppressors will have won nothing

If I were that pigeon that vomits
on the men of bronze
false idols drunken flesh-eaters
feeling the left pectoral
with the right hand
washed by the doves

Who else is capable
of causing amnesia
bestowing deprivation
on those that he governs

Who else can call union
what is discord
to tear away the first
to tear away the best
from the boundaries of all the colonies
who else can call growth
what is regression
construction
what is destruction
the tribes properly pillaged
in the name of the king and of the queen
in the name of the people that are starving to death
in Paris
in London
in Rome
in New York
in Dubai
in Los Angeles
in Dakar
in the name of the people

that are built by the dozen
in Fort-de-France
in Port-au-Prince
in Havana
in Caracas
in Santiago
in Buenos Aires

Aho for joy
Aho for love

Who else knows how to name the lie
to veil it
The city endures in me
sitting on Scavengers Avenue
I watch for elation
the hate that impels me to scream

I watch for the name of the alleys
of the great sea
that lets the poor pass
sheltered from the vultures

War is in me as everywhere.

Here

I remember
memory dragged in the sand
hip broken by the rocks
fingernails broken
pound the ground
wipe my mother's tears
my sister's screams
in the clutches of the storm

I remember
being dishonoured
scratched
twisted
beaten
bled
raped

I remember
having a name
a face
a gaze
a road
a voice
a poem
a cry

I remember
body broken under urine
hip shore
that sleeps
between dogs and wolves

I remember
nausea
fetuses aborted
babies stillborn
orphan children
that were buried
by the Constitution
weeping willows
without voice

The people's autumn
the branches of the trees
breaking under the weight of hail
our forebears without dynasty

Transmission without roots
mirrors of rain
mirrors of river

We no longer sing
we no longer dream
our prophecies lie
on the surface of the rivers
I remember

Here

They will see our underbellies
open up under the weight of the hulls
of black boats

Our cries are of fuel and of peat
mixed with distress
there will be no more anger
there will be no more sadness
there will only be the blazing birch
there will only be despair

The women will scream
redden moon
sun fire
the wolves
pushed back
the shouts

There will be a rustling
between the treetops
heat transformed
under displays of breasts
the universe will generate
a new axis for the fever
they will see our strides
engulf the rhythm

Our sons and our daughters will come out of the reserves
their forebears on their backs
their ancestors in their ears
they will walk toward the South
retrace the North

They will come out of the reserves
new amphibians
crippled humanity

on our coastlines
they will come out of the reserves
and our murky rivers
will recover their flow of long ago

They will have their vigour of yesteryear
the trees will bloom again
like in ancient Syria
I recognize the olive trees
the liveliness of Palestine
its fleshy lips
they will walk miles
Mongolia
Himalaya

Our sons and our daughters will come out of the reserves
will remember
the fabricated poverty
they will crawl to the exits of the reservoirs
of dams of outfitters
they will whisper
je me souviens
they will feel
what is real
what is honorable
they will recall
five centuries later
the first print
of the brown boot
of the devil on the sand
settled between the thighs
of the future America

America America America
I call upon your name
you can no longer look at your mother
you can no longer love your brothers
you can no longer honor your sisters
no grave
will have been given
the bodies abandoned in the void

Our sons and our daughters will come out of the reserves
they will call upon the spirits of the legends
they will pronounce Papakassik^{u}
Tshiuetinishu   Tshakapesh
Tshishikushkueu
the stories will come alive again
on the forest roads
the titans will rise for the cloudy storm
our forebears will shed the tears of love
the rivers of joy
their eyes
the mountains
when they sit watch

To welcome the sun
I will say yes to my birth

The blueberries
grow again

Fires

The people
burnt lands
regenerate
fruit
that gives a taste to the verb exist.

MIGRATION

I am nationless

I have neither land nor territory
the country is born
my blood
my anger

I am its mother

It has denied my face
it has forgotten the milk of my brown breasts
the dreams and the pearls of legends
that I gave it
it no longer remembers my hand
its descendants walk
treading on the name of the earth

It does not recognize
the colour of the tundra
the ferocity of the azure
it walks here as conqueror
five hundred years later
seven generations after

The sons of the peoples that it has enslaved
no longer remember their names

I have not forgotten the kiss of the water
snow solid and white
that lulls to sleep both the earth and its hair

I have not forgotten
my territory made powerful
the joyous taste of its fruits

Pride
and genocide.

I will return
in those stories asphyxiated
by our silent parents
I will go dig up their bodies
I will go dig up my passion
from the depths of my reserve

I go back to the country
bigger than the coureurs des bois
bigger than the premonitions
bigger than the sequoias
my strides land of mine
longer than the pipelines

I go back to the country
as powerful as my grandfathers
as fast as my forebears
as clear-sighted as my grandmothers
as the country itself
it will reveal its herbal tea secrets
the healing of the waters and the earth

I will take back possession of my rights
I will take back possession of my breath
I will take back possession of my waterways
I will name myself Mississippi
Assiniboine
Azueï
Oaxaca
I will have a queen's name
my olden flower

I am
I exist
I have come to bring light to the nations
I have come with the light

I have come back to stay
I have come back to take country
give the land its name.

I
woman among all women
nation among all nations
I take back the name of my ancestors

I have finally found my name again
I have finally found my face again
it sailed on the waters of the oceans
it cried with the boat people
eat my body and drink my blood
here is the sacrifice of the *gran nèg*
that built land of mine with his brow
the sweat on his temples
the calluses on his palms
his teeth in the cane

My name my face
to weep for the rides
Sitting Bull, Tecumseh, Pontiac
to sob for Wounded Knee
Alcatraz, Yucatan, Oka
Elsipuktuk
I have come back with the light

I remember my pain
I remember the needle
that crossed my torso and my chest
I have watered the earth with my breasts
my milk has spread over the whole earth

I know how to say I am
I know how to say the word land
I know how to say the word people

I swear on the language of Africa, my mother
I swear on the arm of Asia, my sister
I swear on the leg of Siberia, my sister
I swear on the foot of Oceania, my sister
I swear on the watery body of America
I will take back my dignity

I will go gather the lover king
I will take him by the hand
I will lead him to the village
five hundred years earlier
seven generations before
we will build a ceremony
the alliance of those who love each other
marry the country in all things
wear the red and blue of the ancestors

I will go gather my son
will carry him on my left arm
dressed in heaven and stars
to enter land of mine
join with the silt

I will tell him in all things
union will be the strength
will reveal to him the secret of my loves
will give him the keys to my city
will bequeath him the chaos of the island

I will whisper my name
in the hollow of his ear
—Anacaona—

so that he remembers
forever

that I am

Land woman

Innu Ishkueu.

I pray
remember
land of mine
land woman
indigenous
sovereign victorious

Land of mine oh
remember
for those come to change your story
reverse the cycle of your rules

My boat over the sea
can no longer hold
my name is unequal
I've had no justice
for too many centuries.

Land of mine oh
do you remember
those come to lie
to deny the mixed blood of our mothers
too little to balance the injustice

Acknowledge the legend
where the hanged queen rises again
standing in the midst of the dead
we will give proper burials
for the celebration
for the memory

Land of mine oh
my cry will know
how to speak
how to scream
how to cradle
how to weep
how to moan

Land of mine oh
remember
my blood
my words

I will come back
for the kiss on my land

I will come back
water my heart
from its streams

I will come back
the dawn will light my passings
will plant my forests

My descendants will say
Nitassinan
Assi

I will come back to name the island
to give it back its history
its name will no longer be unequal

No one can be worthy
of the land
if dignity is not given back
to the women
to the men
to the children

from whom it has been
stolen.

Born in 1991 in Baie-Comeau, Natasha Kanapé Fontaine is Pessamit Innu. Slam poet, painter, actor, and indigenous rights activist, her first book, *N'entre pas dans mon âme avec tes chaussures* (*Do Not Enter My Soul in Your Shoes*), was published in 2012 in French, and in English by Mawenzi House in 2015. In 2013, the original French version won the poetry prize of the Society of Francophone Writers of America. Her second collection, *Manifeste Assi,* was published in French in 2014 by Mémoire d'encrier, and in English by Mawenzi House in 2016. Natasha Kanapé Fontaine lives in Montreal.